MONSTER
Diggers

by Nick Gordon

BELLWETHER MEDIA • MINNEAPOLIS, MN

Note to Librarians, Teachers, and Parents:

Blastoff! Readers are carefully developed by literacy experts and combine standards-based content with developmentally appropriate text.

Level 1 provides the most support through repetition of high-frequency words, light text, predictable sentence patterns, and strong visual support.

Level 2 offers early readers a bit more challenge through varied simple sentences, increased text load, and less repetition of high-frequency words.

Level 3 advances early-fluent readers toward fluency through increased text and concept load, less reliance on visuals, longer sentences, and more literary language.

Level 4 builds reading stamina by providing more text per page, increased use of punctuation, greater variation in sentence patterns, and increasingly challenging vocabulary.

Level 5 encourages children to move from "learning to read" to "reading to learn" by providing even more text, varied writing styles, and less familiar topics.

Whichever book is right for your reader, Blastoff! Readers are the perfect books to build confidence and encourage a love of reading that will last a lifetime!

This edition first published in 2014 by Bellwether Media, Inc.

No part of this publication may be reproduced in whole or in part without written permission of the publisher. For information regarding permission, write to Bellwether Media, Inc., Attention: Permissions Department, 5357 Penn Avenue South, Minneapolis, MN 55419.

Library of Congress Cataloging-in-Publication Data

Gordon, Nick.
  Monster diggers / by Nick Gordon.
    pages cm. – (Blastoff! readers: Monster machines)
  Summary: "Developed by literacy experts for students in kindergarten through grade three, this book introduces extreme diggers to young readers through leveled text and related photos"–Provided by publisher.
  Audience: K-3
  Includes bibliographical references and index.
  ISBN 978-1-60014-937-5 (hardcover : alkaline paper)
  1. Excavating machinery–Juvenile literature. 2. Earthmoving machinery–Juvenile literature. 3. Buckets (Excavating machinery)–Juvenile literature. I. Title.
  TA735.G66 2014
  621.8'65–dc23
                                                                    2013003339

Printed in the United States of America, North Mankato, MN.

Table of Contents

Monster Diggers!

Builders, **loggers**, and **miners** need large diggers.

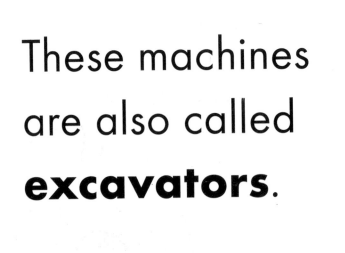

These machines
are also called
excavators.

Most have big
wheels or **tracks**.
They travel on roads
or loose ground.

tracks

Big Buckets

Large diggers have a giant **bucket** or shovel.

bucket

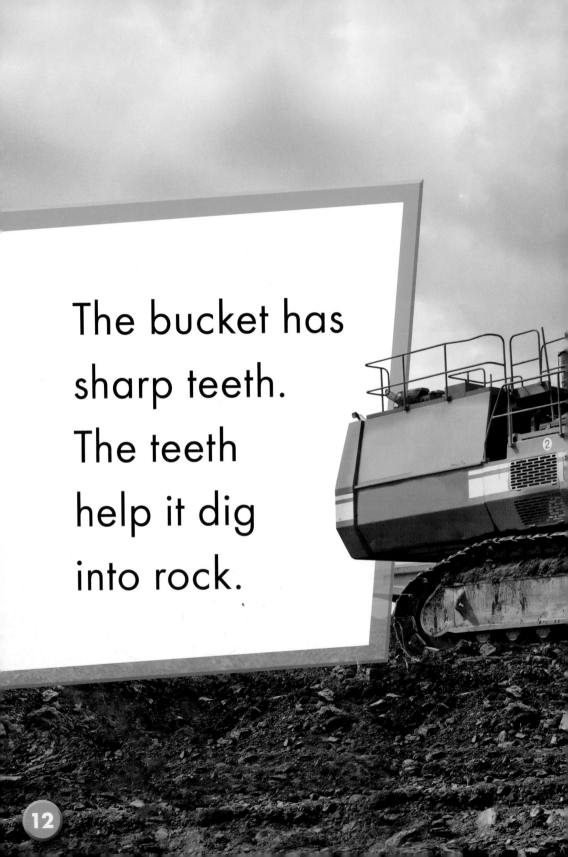

The bucket has
sharp teeth.
The teeth
help it dig
into rock.

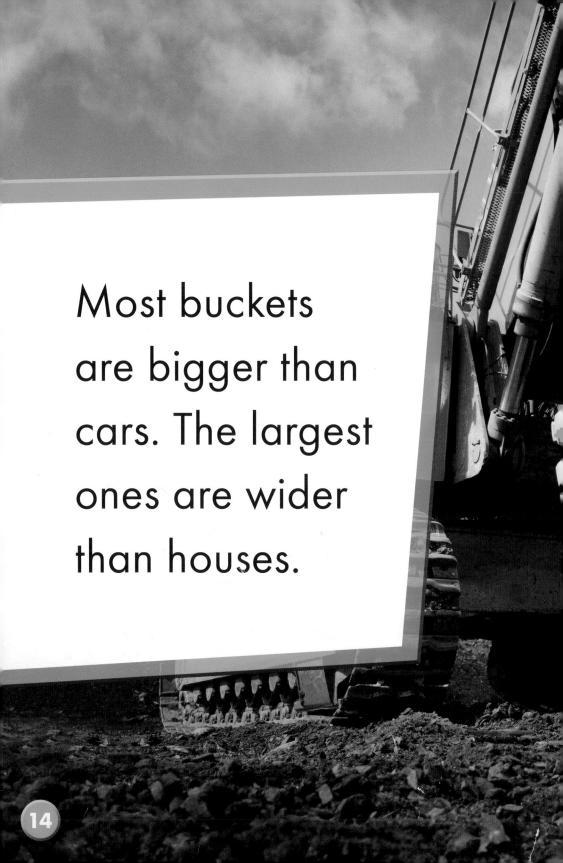

Most buckets are bigger than cars. The largest ones are wider than houses.

Bucket Wheels

Miners use diggers with bucket wheels. The wheels dig as they spin.

bucket wheel

The largest wheels have 18 or 20 buckets.

These diggers
can scoop up
a lot of earth
in one day.
It could fill 96
swimming pools!

Glossary

bucket—the part of a digger that digs into the ground

excavators—machines that dig into the ground; they are also called diggers.

loggers—workers who cut down trees for their wood

miners—workers who collect resources from the ground

tracks—large belts that wrap around wheels; many diggers move on tracks.

To Learn More

AT THE LIBRARY

Addison, D. R. *Diggers at Work*. New York, N.Y.: PowerKids Press, 2009.

Kawa, Katie. *Diggers*. New York, N.Y.: Gareth Stevens Pub., 2012.

Zobel, Derek. *Diggers*. Minneapolis, Minn.: Bellwether Media, 2009.

ON THE WEB

Learning more about diggers is as easy as 1, 2, 3.

1. Go to www.factsurfer.com.

2. Enter "diggers" into the search box.

3. Click the "Surf" button and you will see a list of related Web sites.

With factsurfer.com, finding more information is just a click away.

Index

The images in this book are reproduced through the courtesy of: Inacio pires, front cover; Deere, Inc./ John Deere, pp. 4-5, 6-7; Pic4you/ Getty Images, pp. 8-9; Kaband, pp. 10-11; Monty Rakusen/ Glow Images, pp. 12-13, 14-15; Mik Lav, pp. 16-17; Claffra, pp. 18-19; Hans Georg Elben/ F1online/ Glow Images, pp. 20-21.